Prehistoric

These lizards, toads and turtles, dear,
   with which you love to play,
Were Dinosaurs and Plesiosaurs in prehistoric days.
They fought the armored Ankylosaurs and
   wild Brontosaurus,
Glyptodons and Varanids and hungry Plateosaurus.
Sharklike Ichthyosaurs and flying Pteranodon,
Tyrannosaurus, Kronosaurus and treacherous Trachodon.
Shrieking Archaeopteryx, Triceratops as well,
And those that I cannot pronounce, nor even try
   to spell.
But anyway, they slowly turned to lizards and turtles
   and snakes.
And all the brave and wild prehistoric *people*—
They turned into *us*, for goodness' sakes!

Shel Silverstein

Little People™ Big Book

About DINOSAURS

TIME LIFE for Children™

ALEXANDRIA, VIRGINIA

Table of Contents

When Giants Ruled the Earth

the Apatosaurus leaped over the Allosaurus. Then David ducked as the Stegosaurus jumped over him and the Apatosaurus. All the heavy, brittle bones rattled and clattered and thudded through the moonlit hall.

David was having the time of his life! The Apatosaurus hopped into the air until David almost touched the ceiling. It was like flying! They

41

were leaping higher and higher. David began to worry that their bones would fly apart. As the Apatosaurus soared into the air again, David thought, "I might have to put them back together! That could take a *really* long time!" He began to wish they would slow down.

Just as he wished it, the dinosaur skeletons began to leapfrog a little slower, then still slower. Soon they had stopped completely. David felt relieved. It was fun to fly up in the air, but he was getting tired.

The Apatosaurus knelt down again and David slid off his back. He bowed to his friend. "Here," he said. "I'd like to give you a present." He picked up his red cap and flung it toward the Apatosaurus's head.

"Wake up, David! It's morning!" said Bobby.

David rubbed his eyes. "I had the strangest dream! I dreamed that all the dinosaurs—"

"Did you have fun?" Mrs. Hill, the teacher, asked as she quickly counted heads. "Hurry, now! We have to pack up and leave!"

Later, after the class had left, other people came in to see the great dinosaur skeletons. And nobody was able to figure out how the Apatosaurus had gotten the red cap high atop its bony head.

42

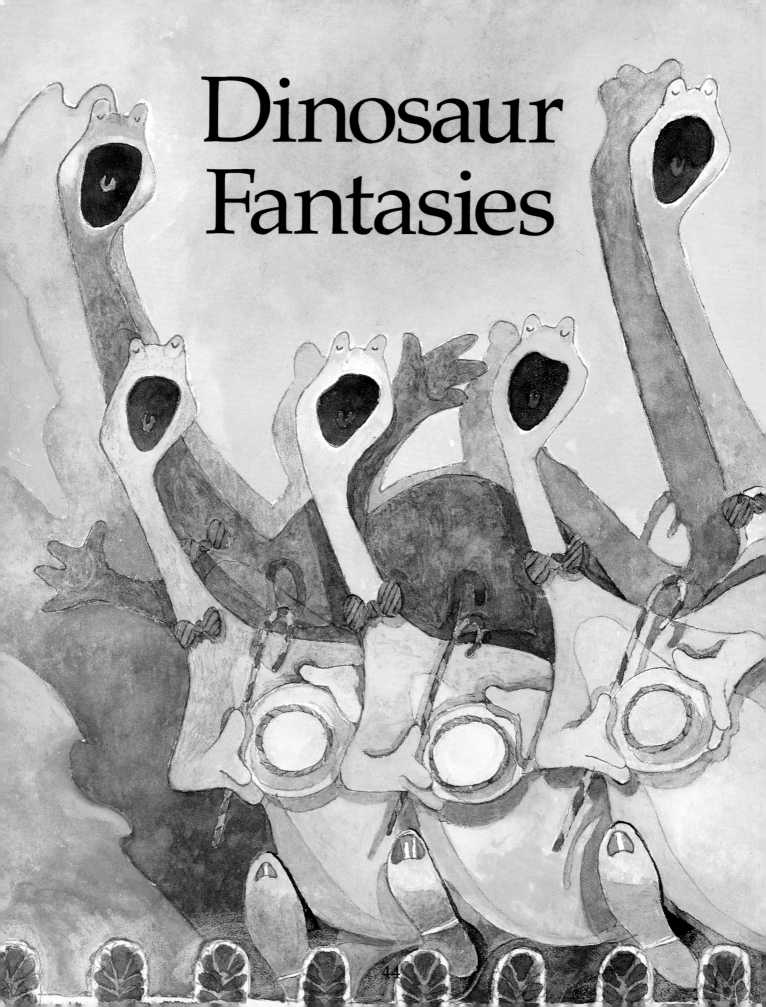

Dinosaur Fantasies

44

Brontosaurus

The giant Brontosaurus
Was a prehistoric chap
With four fat feet to stand on
And a very skinny lap.
The scientists assure us
Of a most amazing thing—
A Brontosaurus blossomed
When he had a chance to sing!

(The bigger Brontosauruses,
Who liked to sing in choruses,
Would close their eyes
and harmonize
And sing most anything.)

They growled and they yowled,
They deedled and they dummed;
They warbled and they whistled,
They howled and they hummed.
They didn't eat, they didn't sleep;
They sang and sang all day.
Now all! you'll find are footprints
Where they tapped the time away!

Gail Kredenser

Dinosaur Dreams

One night I dreamed a dinosaur came,
And gave me a ride to a football game;
When we got there, the game was done,
But we cheered anyway, 'cause our team had won!
Chorus
Dreaming a dream, and playing pretend,
You can meet anyone who can be your friend;
Go anywhere and change the whole scene,
While you're sleeping at night and
    dreaming a dream.

Again the next night, the dinosaur came,
And we went to visit a railroad train;
They didn't see us 'til we boarded the caboose.
Someone yelled out, "Dinosaur's on the loose!"

We walked through the train, my dinosaur and I,
Conductor took our tickets and as he walked by,
Asked, "What's that thing with three horns on his head?"
I said, "Triceratops, and he hasn't been fed!"

So, every night, I rush into bed,
Waiting for my friend with three horns on his head;
I know he's extinct, but not for me,
For when he visits in my dreams he's alive as can be.

Chorus

Dreaming a dream, and playing pretend,
You can meet anyone who can be your friend;
Go anywhere and change the whole scene,
While you're sleeping at night and
   dreaming a dream.

Nancy Silber and Tony Soll

49

Hooray for Dinosaur Day!

by Michael J. Pellowski

S tand still, Rex," Timmy said as he stood on a tall ladder and scrubbed behind the ears of his pet Tyrannosaurus. "I want you looking spick and span for Dinotown's Annual Dinosaur Day Celebration."

Once a year Dinotown held a big dinosaur party. People from near and far brought their pet dinosaurs to town to show them off. There was a grand dinosaur parade down Main Street. There were dinosaur games in the park. And at the end of the day there was even a big dinosaur dance contest in the school gym.

"There. Now you look nice and clean," Timmy said to Rex.

"But I'm still dripping wet," Rex sighed. Like most pets Rex didn't like having a bath.

"You'll have to shake yourself dry," Timmy said. "We don't have a towel big enough to dry you off."

Rex nodded. He lumbered away from the tub and then stood up tall on his hind legs. Then he began to shake. He began to twist and shake. His top half went one way and his bottom half went the other way. He twisted and shook, and shook and twisted. Drops of water went flying every which way. Soon he was completely dry. And Timmy was completely soaked!

"Now we can go to town," Timmy said. "The Grand Parade is about to start. You might even win a prize or trophy this year."

"I doubt it," mumbled Rex as Timmy climbed up on his back. "I'm not good at winning prizes."

When Timmy and Rex reached town, all the dinosaurs were lining up for the Grand Parade. There were Apatosauruses, Stegosauruses,

Triceratops, and lots of others too. Some dinosaurs wore wreaths of flowers. Others were decorated like floats. Leading the parade was the duckbill dinosaur band. Timmy and Rex got in line just as the band began to play. Away went the parade. Up, down and around the streets of Dinotown went the dinosaurs on parade. Buildings shook as they marched by. People on the sidewalks cheered and clapped. Timmy smiled and waved as Rex lumbered by the judging stand.

When the parade was over the mayor of Dinotown announced the awards. A Stegosaurus won a trophy as best-looking dinosaur. His armor plates were so polished they shone like diamonds. A duckbill dinosaur won the prize for having the nicest smile. His one thousand teeth were pearly white. Timmy and Rex didn't win anything.

"Don't feel sad," Timmy said to Rex. "Maybe you'll win a prize at the dinosaur games."

The dinosaur games were held in the park. Rex tried his best, but he didn't win a single contest. Apatosaurus won the dinosaur dash by a neck. A young Allosaurus set a new record in the sack race. Rex almost won the bubblegum blowing contest. He blew the biggest bubble, but the bubble touched one of his pointy teeth and burst. Timmy had to help peel the sticky gum off of Rex's face.

"I'll never win anything," Rex sighed when the games were done.

"Maybe you'll win the dinosaur dance contest," Timmy said.

"But I don't know any dances," Rex groaned.

Timmy smiled. He had an idea. "I know a dance you can do," he said. And he whispered into Rex's ear.

That night people and pet dinosaurs were packed into the school gym. The duckbill dinosaur band provided the music. One by one dinosaurs came on stage and did a dance. There was an Apatosaurus ballet. It was very good, but the Apatosauruses looked a little silly dressed in pink tutus! A Triceratops did an old-fashioned tap dance. His shoes were very shiny. There were even some disco-dancing Diplodocuses.

Finally, it was Rex's turn. Timmy

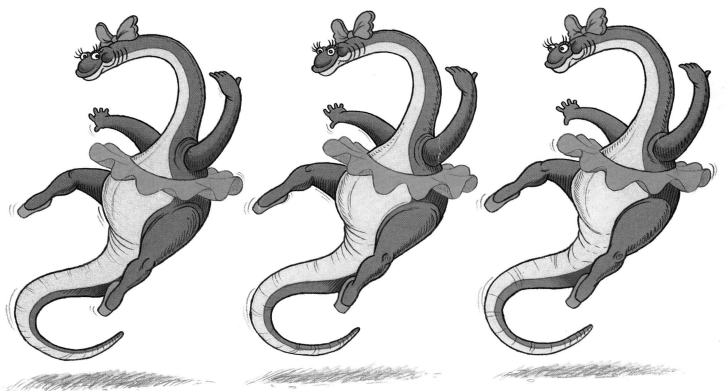

cheered as Rex came out on stage. He hoped their plan would work. The band began to play rock music. Rex stood up tall. He began to twist and shake the way he did after his bath. His top half went one way as his bottom half went the other way. He twisted and shook and shook and twisted.

People clapped and cheered. Dinosaurs whistled and applauded.

"Stop the music!" shouted the mayor of Dinotown. "Rex wins the dinosaur dance contest for doing the Tyrannosaurus Twist." And he handed Rex the biggest trophy of all.

"Hooray!" yelled Timmy as he ran up to hug his pet dinosaur. "Hooray for Rex! Hooray for Dinosaur Day!"

The Dinosore

Poor Dinosore, his body's big,
His tail, it weighs a ton,
His head is full of bones and stone
and when he tries to run

The pounding poundage gets him down.
He gasps and gasps some more.
His aching feet, they have him beat.
That's why he's Dinosore.

Jane Yolen

Dinosaur Jokes and Riddles

What did the Apatosaurus say when the flying reptile took off?

"Look at that dino soar!"

Who won the dinosaur beauty contest?

No one!

What do you get when you cross a dinosaur and a cactus?

The world's biggest porcupine.

What has three horns, eight wheels, and weighs 60,000 pounds?

A Triceratops on roller skates.

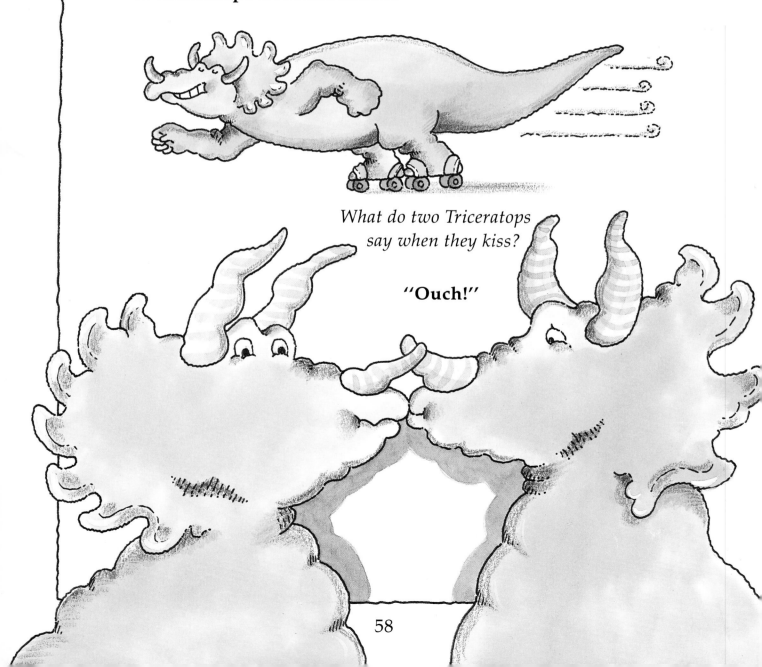

What do two Triceratops say when they kiss?

"Ouch!"

What's gigantic and bumps into mountains?

A Diplodocus playing blindman's bluff.

Which dinosaur is very noisy at night?

The Tyrannosnore.

If the Dinosaurs Were Alive Today

If the dinosaurs were alive today,
they would be so much help!

Can you find the dinosaur that's helping people cross the river?
Can you find the dinosaur that's helping build a tall building?
How about a fire-fighting dinosaur?

And dinosaurs could also be so much fun!
Can you find a dinosaur diving board?
How about the dinosaur swing?
Do you see the dinosaur roller coaster?

Little People™ Big Book About DINOSAURS

TIME-LIFE for CHILDREN™

Publisher: Robert H. Smith
Managing Editor: Neil Kagan
Associate Editors: Jean Burke Crawford,
　　　Patricia Daniels
Marketing Director: Ruth P. Stevens
Promotion Director: Kathleen B. Tresnak
Associate Promotion Director: Jane B. Welihozkiy
Production Manager: Prudence G. Harris
Editorial Consultants: Jacqueline A. Ball,
　　　Sara Mark

PRODUCED BY PARACHUTE PRESS, INC.

Editorial Director: Joan Waricha
Editors: Christopher Medina, Jane Stine, Wendy Wax
Writers: Noelle Anderson, Teddy Gautier,
　　　Michael J. Pellowski, Walter Retan,
　　　Jane Samz, Jean Waricha
Designer: Lillian Lovitt Design
Illustrators: Yvette Banek, Carlos Garzon,
　　　Allan Neuwirth, Earl Norem, John Speirs,
　　　Tad Zar

Time-Life Books Inc. is a wholly owned subsidiary
of the Time Inc. Book Company.

TIME-LIFE is a trademark of Time Warner Inc.
U.S.A.

FISHER-PRICE, LITTLE PEOPLE and AWNING
DESIGN are trademarks of Fisher-Price, Division of
The Quaker Oats Company, and are used under license.

Time-Life Books Inc. offers a wide range of fine
publications, including home video products. For
subscription information, call 1-800-621-7026, or
write TIME-LIFE BOOKS, P.O. Box C-32068, Rich-
mond, Virginia 23261-2068.

ACKNOWLEDGMENTS

Every effort has been made to trace the ownership of all copyrighted material and to secure the necessary
permissions to reprint these selections. If any question arises as to the use of any material, the editor and the
publisher, while expressing regret for any inadvertent error, will make the necessary correction in future
printings.

Grateful acknowledgment is made to the following for permission to reprint copyrighted material: Atheneum
Publishers (a division of Macmillan Publishing Co.) for ''Fossils'' from SOMETHING NEW BEGINS by Lilian
Moore. Copyright © 1967 by Lilian Moore. Curtis Brown Ltd. for ''The Dinosore'' from HOW BEASTLY! by
Jane Yolen. Copyright © 1980 by Jane Yolen. Greenwillow Books (a division of William Morrow & Co.) for
''Long Gone'' from ZOO DOINGS by Jack Prelutsky. Copyright © 1983 by Jack Prelutsky. Harper & Row for
''Prehistoric'' from A LIGHT IN THE ATTIC by Shel Silverstein. Copyright © 1981 by Evil Eye Music, Inc. Gail
Kredenser Mack for ''Brontosaurus.'' Copyright © 1966 by Gail Kredenser Mack. Nancy Silber and Tony Soll for
''Dinosaur Dreams.'' Copyright © 1985 by Nancy Silber and Tony Soll.

Photography credits: Page 30; Chip Clark: Smithsonian Institution. Page 31; Field Museum of Natural History
(Neg #84509c) Chicago. Page 32 top; Neg./Trans. No. PK51 (Photo by Roy C. Andrews). Courtesy Department
Library Services, American Museum of Natural History. Page 32 bottom; Field Museum of Natural History
(Neg #85057c) Chicago. Page 33 top; John Koivula. Page 33 bottom; Field Museum of Natural History (Neg
#G-3T) Chicago.

Library of Congress Cataloging-in-Publication Data

Little people big book about dinosaurs.
　　p.　cm.
　　Summary: A collection of essays, poems, original stories, games, and activities about dinosaurs.
　　ISBN 0-8094-7466-2.—ISBN 0-8094-7467-0 (lib. bdg.)
　　1. Dinosaurs—Literary collections. [1. Dinosaurs—Literary collections.] I. Time-Life for Children (Firm)
PZ5.L7257 1989
　　808'.036—dc20

89-37469
CIP
AC

TIME-LIFE BOOKS
ALEXANDRIA, VIRGINIA

Prehistoric

These lizards, toads and turtles, dear,
   with which you love to play,
Were Dinosaurs and Plesiosaurs in prehistoric days.
They fought the armored Ankylosaurs and
   wild Brontosaurus,
Glyptodons and Varanids and hungry Plateosaurus.
Sharklike Ichthyosaurs and flying Pteranodon,
Tyrannosaurus, Kronosaurus and treacherous Trachodon.
Shrieking Archaeopteryx, Triceratops as well,
And those that I cannot pronounce, nor even try
   to spell.
But anyway, they slowly turned to lizards and turtles
   and snakes.
And all the brave and wild prehistoric *people*—
They turned into *us*, for goodness' sakes!

Shel Silverstein